The Anti-a

recipes for !

anti-stress life

Table of Contents

Introduction

Have you ever considered trying alternative ways to ease your stress and anxiety symptoms other than pills? Stress and anxiety is a very common problem that bothers millions of people worldwide and it is estimated that around 36.5% of diagnosed cases resort on doctor prescribed pills to ease their symptoms. If you are a chronic sufferer of anxiety or have been diagnosed with anxiety recently, then chances are, the only things that you have tried to treat your condition are pills and perhaps random quick fixes like taking deep breaths or exercising. But the question is: do these things really help?

There is one single factor that is actually more important than you can think of--**DIET**! For most of us, the only instant "connection" between anxiety and diet is when we get our daily dose of coffee, only to experience the infamous caffeine jitters afterward. However, there is actually a deeper connection between diet and anxiety than most people realize. As a matter of fact, this connection has been proven again and again through numerous studies. What we choose to eat specifically matters and can have a profound impact on our mental health and well-being. Diet can indirectly influence our mood, mental clarity, energy and stress levels. **It is therefore in our hands to choose a diet that makes us feel better and keeps stress and anxiety levels at bay!**

In this e-book, we will show you how you can do it with everything you need to know about this particular diet as well as 70+ mood-boosting recipes that your body and mind will love. And it won't be hard to follow the diet as all recipes are designed and tested to be healthy and delicious at the same time!

What is the anti-anxiety diet and how it works?

The anti-anxiety diet in a few words aims to ease the symptoms of anxiety and stress (and whatever health problems these are associated with), through the intake of specific nutrients found in certain foods.

The following nutrients have been backed up by various studies as having a positive effect on mental health aspects such as mood, mental clarity, and stress/anxiety levels:

- **Omega-3 fatty acids.** Omega-3 fatty acids are a class of fatty acids (DHA+PHA) that your body can't produce on its own but you must take from your diet as they are essential for various body functions and especially cardiovascular and nervous system health. Some studies have found in particular that cultures who consume sufficient amounts of omega-3 fatty acids in their daily diets suffer from lower levels of anxiety and depression. A 2011 study has also found that the intake of omega-3 fatty acids helps reduce significantly anxiety levels on students who go through academic stress.

- **B-complex vitamins**. B-complex vitamins are essential, water-soluble vitamins that belong to the B-cluster, based on their chemical composition: B1(Thiamin), B2(Riboflavin), B3(Niacin), B5 (Pantothenic Acid),

B6(Pyridoxine), B7(Biotin), B9 (Folic Acid) and B12. The primary role of B-complex vitamins is to help with energy release and the metabolic function of body cells. Evidence has also shown that Niacin, Folic Acid, and B-12 vitamins play a key role in the promotion of good mental health-- their insufficiency is also linked to higher chances of developing mood disorders e.g depression, anxiety, mood swings, etc.

- **Zinc.** Zinc is a naturally occurring mineral that is found in cells in our body but sufficient amounts taken from the diet are also needed as it helps in various metabolic functions. Zinc plays a key role in cell development and division, breakdown of carbs and the metabolic functions of brain cells. Low levels of zinc, which are mostly found in the typical Western diet, have been linked with mood disorders such as anxiety, major depression, and bipolar disorder.

- **Magnesium.** Magnesium is a key mineral involved in over 300 chemical reactions within our bodies. It helps support the immune system, mysokeletal system, and nervous system health among others. Magnesium deficiency has been linked with various conditions including mood disorders e.g anxiety, depression, fatigue as well as poor concentration and memory problems. The mineral is considered by many doctors as a natural "relaxer" as it helps put the person in a more relaxed and stress-free state of mind.

- **Probiotics.** Probiotics are beneficial bacteria that naturally live in our gut and help promote digestive health, immune system health and general system balance. Research has also shown a link between probiotics and mental health--more specifically, some studies have shown that when probiotic cultures are fewer compared to the bad bacteria in our gut, there is an increased chance to develop mental health disorders such as anxiety and depression. Doctors have found that there is an axis between gut flora and the brain, which may improve or worsen mental health problems.

- **Antioxidants**. Antioxidants are essential and non-essential vitamins and minerals that help scavenge free radical damage caused by oxidative stress within the system. Free radical damage is caused by poor diet and lifestyle choices e.g smoking and drinking and is essentially what triggers the aging of our body cells. It has also been found that free radical damage is linked to mood disorders e.g anxiety and depression and brain damage. Antioxidant vitamins and minerals include vitamins A, C, E and K and the minerals copper, zinc, and selenium.

Which foods to eat and which to avoid?

As we have mentioned above, you need to consume foods (and drinks) that have considerable amounts of any of the above anxiety-fighting nutrients. These foods specifically are:

- **Fatty fish and seafood.** Fresh wild-caught fatty fish like salmon, sea bass, sea trout, anchovies, and tuna, are rich sources of omega-3 fatty acids as well as zinc, selenium and Vitamin B-12 which are all known to help reduce anxiety.

- **Eggs.** Eggs are not only packed with good protein and cholesterol, but they also contain considerable amounts of selenium, zinc, and b-complex vitamins that are all useful for busting anxiety.

- **Avocadoes.** Avocados are rich sources of good fat plus C, E, K and some B-complex vitamins and antioxidants that help stop the damaging and stressful effects of free radicals that cause stress.

- **Dark chocolate.** Dark chocolate (around 65-80% cocoa solids) with no sugar added contains very high amounts of magnesium and considerable amounts of iron, selenium, and phosphorus.

- **Forest fruits.** Forest fruits like berries, strawberries, blueberries, cherries, and raspberries are very high in antioxidant nutrients like vitamin C, E, K as well as considerable amounts of folate.

- **Brazil nuts.** Brazil nuts are packed with good amounts of magnesium, phosphorus, and selenium--in fact, a serving of three brazil nuts covers more than 40% of your daily suggested allowance of these nutrients.

- **Dark leafy greens.** Dark leafy greens e.g spinach, kale, and arugula contain good amounts of fiber, vitamin K, Vitamin A, magnesium and folate. They also contain antioxidants (minus the sugar found in fruits).

- **Cruciferous veggies.** Cruciferous veggies like broccoli, cauliflower, cress, cabbage, and Brussels sprouts are good sources of fiber, folate and antioxidant vitamin A, C, and K.

- **Turmeric.** Turmeric has been used for thousands of years for its potent antioxidant multiple health benefits as it contains a massive amount of 300(!) nutrients. The most active compound of Turmeric is called 'Curcumin" and has very strong antioxidant and anti-inflammatory properties.

- **Ginger.** Ginger is a superfood and highly antioxidant plant root that contains many different nutrients e.g Vitamin C, A, potassium and zinc as well as unique antioxidant substances e.g gingerol, shogun and paradol which are super powerful in fighting oxidative stress.

- **Yogurt.** Live yogurt varieties without any sugar or flavors added e.g plain Greek yogurt, are enriched with live probiotic cultures that useful for immunity, good digestion, and good mental health, as we specified before.

- **Beef, pork or chicken liver.** Animal liver is probably the richest animal source of mood and nervous system boosting B-complex vitamins like folate and B-12. B-12 the only B-complex vitamin that is found exclusively on animal sources. e.g meat and dairy.

- **Fermented foods.** Fermented foods such as kimchi, sauerkraut, kombucha, and random pickled veggies are made through a process called "fermentation" which produces beneficial probiotic bacteria as a result.

In addition to the above, most nuts, sprouts, and seeds also contain significant amounts of protein, fiber, and antioxidants. Meats are also great as long as they come from fresh and preferably organic sources.

 Of course, you don't have to eat any of the above foods only as many e.g fish and avocados are expensive and not always available but you can mix them up with other foods e.g meat or wholegrain pasta to prepare complete meals. See our recipe section for exact ways to pair these up.

Now, when it comes to foods that you should avoid, here is a list of foods that not only help you ease your anxiety symptoms, they may actually make matters worse:

- **Caffeine** (over 400mg/day). Caffeine is not exactly damaging for people who suffer from anxiety but high doses that surpass 400mg/day can lead to sudden energy loss, anxiety and abnormal heart palpitations.

- **Sugar/sweets**. Sugar and sweets containing processed white sugar are not only damaging for your body, but they can also hurt your brain and mental health too. Sugar specifically causes a sudden spike in blood glucose and this action slows down normal cognitive function and also hinders normal mood levels.

- **Processed foods.** Processed foods and especially in foods, processed meat e.g salami, fast food, and frozen/microwave meals contain many harmful preservatives, chemicals e.g flavor enhancers and even heavy metals that are neurotoxic. This means that they are capable of attacking the nervous system and brain cells and actually force them to die over time. This is perhaps the most dangerous category of all as their effects are more damaging and lasting compared to any other food group on this list.

- **Bread and pasta byproducts**. Bread and pasta are ok when eaten 2-3 times a week and especially if they are wholegrain but white bread, pasta and all products produced by white flour contain gluten and bad carbs that convert into glucose and cause mood problems.

Drinks that contain added amounts of sugar e.g sodas, colas, or fruit cocktails, alcoholic drinks, and ready-made packed smoothies should also be avoided.

In general, any product that is packed and contains sugar or toxic sugar alternatives e.g aspartame should be avoided.

Anti-anxiety Diet FAQS

If you are a beginner in the anti-anxiety diet, chances are you have some questions on how to make the most of this diet as well as some possible mistakes to avoid. Here are the most common ones:

Q: *"Will my anti-anxiety medicine interfere with this diet?"*

A: In most cases, no. The anti-anxiety diet and nearly all of its ideal foods are perfectly safe for those who take anti-anxiety medicine such as sertraline, vilazodone, or citalopram. However, certain herbs like ginger or turmeric should not be taken at the same time with anti-anxiety herbs as they may interfere with the drug's action. When in doubt, ask your doctor to find out exactly what you should avoid when taking certain drugs.

Q: *Does cooking method matter in an anti-anxiety diet?*

A: Yes. Cooking method matters very much like the way you choose to cook the food can either improve or damage the nutritional value you get from each meal. Healthy cooking involved grilling, broiling, poaching, boiling and slow-cooking with minimal oil. Deep-frying and overcooking foods not only destroy the nutrients you get from your food, but they also release harmful toxic substances that are harmful to your system in general.

Q: Do I have to limit my daily amount of calories?

A: Generally speaking, calories don't really matter when it comes to an anti-anxiety diet unless you also have a weight or any other health problem that advises keeping your daily calorie intake up to a certain level. It's best though to avoid in general overeating and consuming more than 3K calories per day to avoid fat gain and other health problems.

Q: Should I buy organic foods in an anti-anxiety diet?

A: There is no need to buy all organic foods but it's best to buy mostly organic foods if your budget allows you to do so. Meats and fish should ideally come from organic farm-raised or wild-caught resources that do not contain any hormones and toxic chemicals. Some fruits and veggies like peaches, apples, grapes, celery, sweet bell peppers, lettuce, and spinach should be preferably organic as they tend to absorb the highest amount of pesticides when not organic. However, bananas, avocados, carrots, pineapple, onions, eggplants, squash, sweet peas, and asparagus, don't have to be organic as they naturally absorb the least amount of pesticides, because of their thick skin and structure.

Q: Are there any other lifestyle changes that I should make along with the diet?

A: Yes. While following a good diet that fights anxiety and boosts overall health is the most important lifestyle change you need to make, making other secondary lifestyle changes will amplify and fasten the results you will get. Some of these are also helpful enough alone for combating anxiety: exercising, meditation, deep breathing techniques, etc. Try to stay away from addictive substances like alcohol, smoking products, and high doses laxative pills as this wreak havoc on the nervous system and sabotage all your diet efforts.

Q: *Do I need to take supplements with this diet?*

A: Taking supplements when following this diet is not necessary, especially if you try to eat a wide range of recipes and meals--while each of the following recipes contains sufficient amounts of anxiety-busting ingredients, it's best to incorporate a variety of these in your weekly diet plan so you can get more nutrients out of your diet. Still, supplements in balanced and not excessive doses may not hurt. In most cases though, doctors and nutritionists recommend that you take at least 80% of your nutrients through diet and only use supplements to complement your diet--not as replacements.

Recipes

Breakfast recipes

Banana Chia Pudding

A dessert-like sweet breakfast for banana lovers, fortified with omega-3 enriched chia seeds for a long-lasting and positive energy boost. For best results make this ahead and leave in the fridge overnight.

Servings: 2

Ingredients:
- 2 medium ripe bananas
- 1 ½ cup of unsweetened coconut milk
- 4 tbsp of chia seeds
- 1 tsp of vanilla extract
- ½ tsp cinnamon
- 1 tbsp of chopped pecans (optionally), for garnish

Method:
- Mesh one banana with a fork. Combine with the chia seeds, coconut milk, vanilla extract and cinnamon in a bowl.
- Transfer the banana/chia seed mixture in a medium-size mason jar, cover and leave in the fridge for at least 4 hours or overnight.
- Slice the second banana into thin slices and add on top. Add optionally the chopped pecans. Serve chilled.

Nutritional info per serving:
Calories: 624kcal, Carbs: 44.4g, Protein: 8.2g., Fat:50.5g,
Dietary Fiber: 12.9g.

Avocado & Egg Toast

A hearty toast recipe packed with a rich flavor of avocados, spices, and boiled eggs for extra protein and nutrients.

Servings: 1

Total cooking time: 10 minutes

Ingredients:

- 1 ripe avocado, peeled and halved
- 1 egg
- 1 long whole-wheat toast (around 5-6" in length)
- ½ tsp of paprika
- ½ tsp cumin
- 1 tsp of lemon juice
- ½ tsp black sesame seeds
- ½ salt
- 1 tsp olive oil

Method:

- Mash the avocado with a fork or process in a blender with spices, salt, olive oil, and lemon juice. You should end up with a rich green cream.
- Boil the egg in boiling water for 7-8 minutes (for medium doneness). Let rest for 2-3 minutes and peel. Cut into 5-6 thin round slices with a sharp knife.
- Toast your bread in the toaster. Take a spoon and spread first with the avocado mixture. Top with the egg slices and sprinkle with the sesame seeds on top.

Nutritional info per serving:
Calories: 518kcal, Carbs: 31.9g, Protein: 14.28g, Fat: 40.4g, Dietary Fiber: 14.28g.

Chinese Spice Egg-white Omelette

A light and fluffy egg white omelet with a hint of Chinese spices for extra flavor. Perfect for weight loss as well.

Servings: 1

Total cooking time: 2 minutes

Ingredients:

- 2 large egg whites
- 1 tbsp of water
- ½ red bell pepper, diced
- 1 spring onion, sliced
- ½ tsp of Chinese 5-spice powder
- ½ tsp of salt
- ½ tsp of pepper
- 1 tbsp of olive oil

Method:

- Beat the egg whites with the water in a bowl until fluffy and smooth.
- Add the Chinese-spice, sugar,pepper, and salt.
- Place a small shallow skillet over medium heat and add olive oil. Add the spring onion and pepper dices and saute for a couple of minutes.
- Add the eggs and allow them to set/cook fully (with the lid on).
- Serve warm.

Nutritional info per serving:
Calories: 174 kcal, Carbs: 5.36g, Protein: 7.53g, Fat: 13.77g, Dietary Fiber:0.7g.

Oatmeal & Berry Pancakes

An easy yet incredibly delicious pancake recipe with just 4 ingredients--great with honey and agave syrup.

Servings: 4

Total cooking time: 8 minutes

Ingredients:
- ½ cup of rolled oats
- ⅓ cup of rice milk
- 1 tbsp of honey
- ¼ cup blueberries

Method:
- Blend all the ingredients in a food processor until you end up with a creamy paste.
- Spray a small skillet with cooking spray and spoon off the mixture in small circle parts. Use the spoon to spread evenly the mixture in the center of the pan, making small round pancakes (around 3-4 inches in diameter). Cook for 1 minute on one side and then flip with a spatula.
- Repeat all the above steps to finish off the mixture.

Tip: If the mixture is too liquid or hard to flip, add more oats.

Nutritional info per serving:
Calories: 240kcal, Carbs: 61.2, Protein:8.9g, Fat: 4.4g, Dietary Fiber: 8.5g

Breakfast Egg White Wrap

A light egg wrap with delicious egg white feeling, lettuce and a touch of heat with a bit sriracha sauce. Great as a snack too.

Servings: 2

Total cooking time: 2-3 minutes

Ingredients:

- 4 egg whites
- 1 tbsp of mild mustard
- 1 tsp of paprika powder
- 2 small corn tortillas (around 6 inches each)
- 1 lettuce leaf, cut in half
- 2 tbsp of sriracha sauce
- 1 tbsp of olive oil
- Salt
- Pepper

Method:

- Beat the egg whites with the mustard and paprika powder and a very little salt and pepper in a bowl.
- Heat the olive oil in the skillet over medium heat and add the egg mixture. Scramble the eggs with a spatula and once cooked and solid, remove from the heat.
- Lay one lettuce piece on the top inside part of each tortilla and fill with the egg mixture on top, making sure it is distributed evenly. Add one tbsp of sriracha sauce over each and begin to fold the

tortillas from the sides, as if you are making a burrito.

- Wrap in paper and serve hot or cold.

Nutritional info per serving:
Calories: 169kcal, Carbs: 15.6g, Protein:9.7g, Fat: 8g, Dietary Fiber: 2.9g

Ultimate Berry Breakfast smoothie

A rich breakfast smoothie for a quick energy boost in the morning. This zingy purple smoothie is also full of good-for-you antioxidants.

Servings: 1

Total cooking time: 1 minute

Ingredients:

- ½ cup of frozen mixed berries e.g strawberries, blueberries
- 1 cup of rice milk
- 1tsp of vanilla extract
- 1 tbsp of honey
- 1 tbsp (optional)of pure protein powder

Method:
- Blend all the ingredients in a blender until smooth.
- Serve chilled with crushed ice or ice cubes on top.

Nutritional info per serving:
Calories: 231kcal, Carbs:45.9g, Protein: 5.7g, Fat: 2.5g, Dietary Fiber: 2.9g

Mustard & Honey Turkey Sausage

Servings: 4

Total cooking time: 5-7 minutes

Ingredients:

- 1 pound of ground lean turkey (around 85% lean)
- 1 tbsp of mustard
- 1 tbsp of honey
- 1 tsp of thyme
- 1 clove of garlic, crushed
- 1 tbsp of olive oil
- 1 tsp of salt
- Pepper

Method:
- Combine all ingredients in a bowl and form with your hands 4 medium flat patties.
- Heat a medium skillet or grilling pan and spray with some cooking spray.
- Cook over medium heat for around 2 minutes on each side. (You will know once they are cooked if they do not feel soft and tender when pressed in the center).
- Serve hot.

Nutritional info per serving:
Calories: 220kcal, Carbs: 5g, Protein: 21.4g, Fat:12.9g
Dietary Fiber: 0.3g

Breakfast Egg Bake

A hearty breakfast bake with peppers, bread, and leftover chicken. Great for all the family and guests too.

Servings: 6

Total cooking time: 40 minutes

Ingredients:

- 1 cup of cooked chicken flesh, cut in small pieces
- 1 red bell pepper, sliced
- 3 spring onions, sliced
- 2 slices of cooked bacon, chopped
- 4 large egg whites
- 1 whole egg
- 2 tbsp of heavy cream
- 1 tsp of paprika
- ½ tsp garlic powder
- 3 slices of whole wheat bread (for toasting), cubed
- ½ cup of cheddar cheese, shredded
- 1 tsp of salt
- Pepper

Method:
- Grease the bottom of a small-medium baking pan (around 3 quarts) with some cooking spray.
- Preheat the oven at 320F/175C.
- While the oven heats beat the eggs with the heavy cream, paprika, garlic powder, salt, and pepper.

- Begin to layer all the rest of the ingredients inside the baking pan and stir to distribute everything evenly.
- Add the egg mixture on top, stir and sprinkle with the shredded cheddar cheese on top.
- Cook in the oven for 30-35 minutes.
- Let chill for 10 minutes before serving.

Nutritional info per serving:
Calories:119kcal, Carbs: 9.5g, Protein: 15.5g, Fat:10.8, Dietary Fiber: 1.7g

Zucchini Fritters

Lovely savory breakfast with shredded zucchini when you need something hearty and delicious in the morning.

Servings: 2 (4 small fritters)

Total cooking time: 5 minutes

Ingredients:

- 1 large zucchini, shredded
- 3 egg whites
- 2 tbsp of white flour
- 1 tsp of dill
- ½ tsp salt
- 1 tsp of pepper
- 2 tbsp of olive oil

Method:

- Beat the eggs with a hand mixer or an egg whisk until fluffy and white.
- Add the shredded zucchini and fold gently in, using a spatula.
- Add the dill, salt/pepper, and flour. Stir gently.
- Grease a shallow skillet with the olive oil (or cooking spray) and make one round fritter each time (around 3 inches in diameter) with the help of a large spoon.
- Cook until each side has turned golden brown (around 2 minutes from each side). Repeat the above step until you finish with the mixture.
- Serve warm.

Nutritional info per serving:
Calories: 181kcal, Carbs:7.8g, Protein:6.7g, Fat: 13.8g,
Dietary Fiber: 0.8g

4-ingredient Energy Balls

A 4-ingredient energy ball that is nut-free yet very rich in flavor and texture. Make these little balls as a breakfast or snack on the go, in only 2 minutes.

Servings: 16 balls

Total cooking time: 2 minutes

Ingredients:

- 1 cup of oats
- ⅓ cup tahini paste
- 1 tbsp of maple syrup
- ½ cup of pitted dates

Method:

- Pulse the dates in a food processor until they become a coarse crumb.
- Add the tahini paste and maple syrup and pulse until you get a dough-like mixture.
- Take the mixture with your hands and form 1-2 inch balls.
- Store in the fridge for up to a week.

Nutritional info per serving:

Calories:64kcal, Carbs:9.8g, Protein:2.1g, Fat:3.4g, Dietary Fiber:1.8g

Blueberry Bagels

Who doesn't love bagels? Now, you can make this dairy-free alternative without any guilt as this recipe is gluten-free and very low in sugar.

Servings: 12

Total cooking time: 45 minutes

Ingredients:

- 2 cups of water at room temperature
- 5 cups of almond flour
- 2 packs of dry active yeast
- 3 tbsp of sugar
- 2 cups of fresh blueberries
- ¼ cup cornmeal
- 1 tsp of salt
- 10 cups of water

Method:
1. In a medium bowl mix together the warm water with the yeast and sugar and let activate for 5 minutes or until it has formed bubbles on top.
2. Add the cups of almond flour and salt in parts, and stir gently until the mixture resembles a soft dough. Add in the blueberries and stir gently.
3. Spread out the dough in a lightly flour-dusted flat surface and knead with your hands until the dough is flexible and stretchable.
4. Place the dough in a big bowl, cover with a tablecloth and let rise in volume for approx. 50 minutes to an hour (at room temperature).
5. Preheat the oven at 400F/190C.

6. Lightly grease a large baking pan.
7. Flatten the dough and split into 12 equal pieces. Make a ball with your fingers and make a hole in the center of each using your fingers as well. The hole should be the size of a big coin e.g dime. Place them over a parchment paper layer, cover with a tablecloth and let rise in volume for an extra 25 minutes.
8. Grease a separating baking pan and dust with cornmeal. Add 10 cups of water in a large pot to boil. Boil in batches of 3-4 at a time. Boil each batch until they rise on top (approx. 5 minutes).
9. Transfer all the boiled bagels in the prepared and dusted baking pan.
10. Bake for 35 minutes. Flip during the first 10 minutes.
11. Serve at room temperature.

Nutritional info per serving:
Calories: 228kcal, Carbs:55.6g, Protein:1.06g, Fat:0.2g, Dietary Fiber: 2.9g

Feta Cheese & Olive Frittata

A tasty and light frittata inspired by the Mediterranean flavors of spinach, olives, and feta cheese.

Servings: 2

Total cooking time: 10-12 minutes

Ingredients:
- 5 egg whites
- 1 egg yolk
- 1 cup spinach
- 1 tsp of baking powder
- ⅓ cup pitted black olives
- ⅓ cup crumbled feta cheese
- 1 tsp of dried oregano
- ½ tsp of salt
- 2 tbsp of olive oil
- Pepper

Method:
1. Beat the egg whites with the egg yolk until fluffy and smooth.
2. Add in the olives and crumbled feta cheese and stir gently. Season with the oregano, salt, and pepper.
3. Grease a medium deep skillet (around 8") with the olive oil. Add the spinach to wilt for 1 minute and add the egg mixture.
4. Bake in the oven for 10 minutes.
5. Serve warm and cut into 2 parts or 4-6 triangles before serving.

Nutritional info per serving:

Calories:286kcal, Carbs:5.3g, Protein:14.5g, Fat:23.3g, Dietary Fiber:1.3g

Balsamic Yogurt & Fruit Parfait

A fresh and fruity breakfast that is perfect for summer months--the taste of the yogurt and fruits is also amplified by the rich and sweet flavor of balsamic vinegar syrup.

Servings: 2

Total cooking time: 2 minutes

Ingredients:

- 1 ½ cups of vanilla-flavored soy yogurt
- 1 green apple, cut into small pieces
- 6 cherries, pitted and halved
- 2 tbsp of maple syrup
- 3 tbsp of balsamic vinegar

Method:

1. Distribute the vanilla yogurt into 2 glass mason jars. Add the apple pieces and cherries on top.
2. In a small saucepan, combine the brown sugar with the balsamic vinegar. Let simmer until sugar is melted and the mixture becomes a thin syrup.
3. Drizzle the syrup with a spoon on top of the yogurt and fruits.
4. Serve chilled.

Nutritional info per serving:
Calories: 277 kcal, Carbs: 58.4g, Protein:5.07g, Fat: 3.17g, Dietary Fiber: 3.3g

Poached Eggs in Peppers

An incredibly easy yet flavorful and colorful recipe with peppers, eggs, and live ricotta cheese.

Servings:2

Total cooking time: 12 minutes

Ingredients:

- 2 small green bell peppers
- 2 large eggs
- 2 tbsp ricotta cheese
- 1 tsp of mint
- Drizzle of olive oil
- Salt
- Pepper

Method:

1. Slice off the top of each pepper and remove the seeds.
2. Lightly season the inside part with salt and pepper and drizzle with olive oil.
3. Add one egg white on each pepper and top with 1 tbsp of ricotta cheese and ½ tsp of mint on each.
4. Bake in the oven at 400F/200C for 10-12 minutes.
5. Serve warm.

Nutritional info per serving:

Calories: 156kcal, Carbs: 7.2g, Protein: 9.2gg, Fat:10.4g, Dietary Fiber: 24g

Fresh Green Smoothie

A quick energizing and detoxifying smoothie that is full of several beneficial nutrients for your digestive and nervous system.

Servings: 1

Total cooking time:2 minutes

Ingredients:

- 1 small stalk of celery, sliced
- 1 green apple, skinned and seeded
- 1 tsp of ginger powder
- 1 cup of plain water
- 1 tsp of honey
- 1/2 cup ice

Method:

1. Blend all the ingredients in a blender until smooth.
2. Serve chilled.

Nutritional info per serving:

Calories:121kcal, Carbs: 31.84g, Protein: 0.65g, Fat:0g, Dietary Fiber: 4.7g.

Soda Bread Biscuits

A versatile recipe for making fluffy and satisfying American biscuits that you can enjoy with your favorite berry jam, for breakfast or a snack.

Servings: 12 biscuits

Total cooking time: 20 minutes

Ingredients:

- 3 cups of oat flour
- 1 stick of unsalted butter, cut into squares
- 1 tsp of baking soda
- ½ tsp of salt
- 2 tsp of caraway seeds (optional)
- ½ cup of raisins
- 1 ¼ cups of half and half

Method:

1. Preheat the oven at 400F/195C and grease a 12 unit muffin pan.
2. Combine all dry ingredients in a mixing bowl.
3. Add the butter squares and incorporate the butter with the dry mixture gently with your hands until you end up with a coarse dough.
4. Add the raisins and/or caraway seeds and work again with your fingers.
5. Make a well in the middle of the mixture and add the half and half. Use a spoon to stir everything, working from the sides to the center.
6. Use your hands to knead and form the mixture into a slightly sticky and loose but not too dry nor too moist.

7. Divide the dough into 12 muffin tins.
8. Bake for 13-15 minutes.
9. Once baked, let chill at room temperature for 10 minutes and serve.

Nutritional info per serving:
Calories: 176kcal, Carbs: 26.2g, Protein: 4.23g, Fat:g6.64 Dietary Fiber: 2.1g

Matcha Pancakes

An Instagram-worthy pancake recipe that utilizes the famous super antioxidant matcha/green tea powder for a vibrant and fresh color and flavor.

Servings: 8

Total cooking time: 15 minutes

Ingredients:

- 2 whole eggs
- ⅔ cup of rice milk
- ¼ cup of coconut sugar
- ¼ cup of vegetable oil
- 1 tsp of vanilla extract
- ½ cup of cornflour
- 1 tbsp of baking powder
- 2 tbsp of matcha powder
- ⅛ tsp salt

Method:

1. Combine the eggs, rice milk, 2 tbsp of the vegetable oil, vanilla extract, and sugar.
2. Add all the dry ingredients (matcha, cornflour, salt, baking powder) into the liquid mixture and whisk.
3. Heat a small skillet with the remaining vegetable oil. Add ¼ cup of the mixture each time and use a spatula if necessary to even out each pancake. Pancakes should be small and round.
4. Cook 1 minute on each side and then flip carefully with a spatula. Repeat the above two steps until all pancake butter has run out.

5. Serve the pancakes warm and top optionally with some raspberries or maple syrup.

Nutritional info per serving:
Calories: 128kcal, Carbs:12g, Protein: 1.9g, Fat:8.3g
Dietary Fiber:0.7g

Lunch recipes

Avocado, Carrot & Ginger Salad

A superfood zesty salad that combines ideally the flavors of avocado, carrot, and ginger. You can either prepare it fresh or keep it overnight with the dressing separately and eat it for lunch at work or school.

Servings: 4

Total cooking time: 5 minutes

Ingredients:

- 1 large carrot, peeled and roughly chopped
- 1 ripe avocado, sliced
- 1 small shallot, sliced
- ¼ red onion, thinly sliced
- 1 small head of lettuce, sliced
- 2 tbsp sweet miso sauce
- 2 tbsp ginger, thinly chopped
- 2 tbsp rice vinegar
- 2 tbsp toasted sesame oil
- ¼ grapeseed oil
- 2 tbsp water

Method:
1. Combine all the veggies together with the ginger and toss.
2. In a small bowl, mix the miso sauce with the rice vinegar, sesame oil, grapeseed oil, and water.
3. Pour the dressing over the salad and serve.

Nutritional info per serving:

Calories: 317kcal, Carbs: 14.7g, Protein: 3.8g,Fat: 28.5g, Dietary Fiber: 2.4g.

Quick BBQ Chicken Pizza

A quick and easy pizza recipe made with gluten-free corn tortillas, leftover chicken and of course the spicy and smoked flavors of barbeque sauce.

Servings: 2

Total cooking time:20 minutes

Ingredients:

- 2 medium-sized corn tortillas (around 8 inches each)
- 4 oz. of leftover cooked chicken, shredded
- 2 tbsp of spicy barbeque sauce
- 1 large red onion, sliced
- ¼ cup shredded Monterey jack cheese

Method:

4. Spread two tbsp of barbeque sauce over each tortilla.
5. Top with the shredded chicken and a few onion slices over each tortilla.
6. Finally, sprinkle and distribute the cheese on the tortillas.
7. Bake in the oven at 300F/160C for 12-15 minutes.

Nutritional info per serving:
Calories: 229 kcal, Carbs: 19.1g, Fat:8.1m Dietary Fiber: 3.1g.

Broccoli, Chicken & Almond Saute

Not everyone likes broccoli but there are some recipes like this one that makes broccoli eating totally enjoying and not a chore. This balanced meal contains good amounts of protein and antioxidants with minimal bad fats.

Servings: 4

Total Cooking Time: 20 minutes

Ingredients:

- ½ pound lean chicken breast
- 1 pound broccoli florets
- 1 tbsp of chicken seasoning
- 1 tbsp olive oil
- ¼ tsp chili flakes
- ½ cup toasted almonds, chopped
- 3 cups lightly salted water
- 1 tsp sesame oil
- 1 tbsp soy sauce
- Salt
- Pepper

Method:
1. Place salted water to boil. Add the broccoli florets and let cook for around 7-8 minutes. Drain and set aside.
2. While the broccoli is boiling, season the chicken breasts with the seasoning and chili flakes. Add salt and pepper to taste.
3. Rub with the olive oil and cook in a grilling pan until there are no longer pink inside and outside.

Remove from the heat, rest and slice into thick slices.
4. Heat the sesame oil in a wok or deep pan and add the chicken, cooked broccoli, and chopped almonds. Add soy sauce and cook everything for another 2 minutes.

Nutritional info per serving:
Calories: 108kcal, Carbs: 4.91g, Protein: 10.1g, Fat: 6.1g Dietary Fiber: 2.1g

Butter Crab Risotto

A hearty risotto recipe made with real or imitation crab meat sauteed with shallots in butter. Very creamy,aromatic,and flavorful.

Servings: 2

Total cooking time: 18-20 minutes

Ingredients:

- ⅔ cup white risotto rice
- ½ cup white crabmeat
- 2 tbsp of butter
- 2 long shallots, sliced
- ¼ cup white wine
- 2 ½ cups of low sodium chicken stock
- 1 tbsp of parmesan cheese, grated
- 1 tsp of salt
- ½ tsp of nutmeg

Method:

1. Melt 1 tbsp of butter in a deep skillet and once the butter is melted, add the crabmeat and shallots. Add the white wine and let cook until all vine is evaporated.
2. Add the rice and give everything a good stir. Slowly incorporate the fish stock into the rice mixture in small parts of half a cup each time, while stirring. Stir for around a minute before you add the next part.
3. Once all the chicken stock has been added, cover the lid of the skillet and let cook until rice is cooked but creamy.

4. Add the remaining 1 tbsp of butter in the mix, just a few moments before you take the risotto off the heat to add even more creaminess. Season with the salt and nutmeg.
5. Sprinkle some parmesan cheese and serve.

Nutritional info per serving:
Calories: 460kcal, Carbs: 60.7g, Protein: 11.6g, Fat: 14.5g, Dietary Fiber: 2.3g

Kale, Apple & Goat Cheese Salad

A lovely rustic salad with a bit of crunch that is perfect for all seasons--plus it's less than 250 calories for those that wish to lose weight too.

Servings: 2

Total cooking time: 5 minutes

Ingredients:

- 1 large bunch of kale
- 1 medium green apple, sliced
- 2 oz. of goat cheese, crumbled
- ⅓ cup gluten-free bread croutons
- 2 tbsp of dijon mustard
- 1 tbsp of olive oil
- 1 tbsp of lemon
- 1 tsp of honey
- ½ tsp thyme
- Salt/Pepper

Method:
1. Cut kale into big and rough pieces (with your hands or with a knife).
2. Add the apple sliced and goat cheese and toss everything together.
3. In a small bowl or a food processor mix the olive oil, lemon, mustard, honey, thyme, salt, and pepper until smooth.
4. Pour the dressing over the salad and toss well.
5. Add the croutons on top and lightly toss again.
6. Serve.

Nutritional info per serving:

Calories: 285 kcal, Carbs: 22.6g, Protein: 10.7g, Fat: 18g, Dietary Fiber: 3.9g

Pinto Bean Burger Patties

If you fancy a quick vegan alternative of the ordinary burger that will keep you full for hours, this is the recipe to go for. This is also full of vegan protein, phosphorus and a bit of iron.

Servings: 4

Total cooking time: 10 minutes

Ingredients:

- 1 jar of kidney beans (around 14.5 oz), drained
- 2 large spring onions, chopped
- 2 tbsp gluten-free breadcrumbs
- 1 tbsp of olive oil (plus a drizzle for greasing your hands)
- 1 tsp Italian seasoning
- 2 tbsp fresh parsley, chopped
- Salt/Pepper

Method:
1. Smash the kidney beans with a fork until you end up with a mushy paste (the beans don't have to be completely smashed).
2. In a small skillet saute the onions with the olive oil until transparent.
3. Add the sauteed onions to the mashed beans. Stir and add the breadcrumbs, the Italian seasoning, and the parsley. Season with salt and pepper.

4. Grease your hands with some extra olive oil and take the mixture to form some medium flat patties with your hand (around 4-5 inches each).
5. Bake in a non-stick grilling pan for 3 minutes on each side.
6. Serve optionally with some lettuce salad.

Nutritional info per serving:
Calories: 386kcal, Carbs: 65.1g, Protein: 23.1g, Fat:4.6g, Dietary Fiber: 15.9g

Jalapeno Popper Mushrooms

If you have an upcoming family or guest party, this delicious lunch/finger food is going to be a total hit as it combines the rich flavor and texture of the mushrooms with 2 kinds of cheese and jalapenos for extra heat and freshness.

Servings: 8

Total cooking time: 25 minutes

Ingredients:

- 20 small white mushrooms, cleaned and stems trimmed
- 8 oz. cream cheese, at room temperature
- ⅔ cup shredded cheddar cheese
- 4 oz. can or jar jalapenos, finely chopped
- 2 cloves of garlic, minced
- A drizzle of olive oil
- Salt
- Pepper

Method:

1. Combine the cream cheese with half of the cheddar cheese, garlic and jalapenos. Season lightly with salt and pepper and stir everything together.
2. Drizzle the mushrooms lightly with the olive oil and begin stuffing the mushrooms with the mixture using a spoon (around 1 tbsp for each mushroom).
3. Sprinkle the remaining cheddar cheese on top of the mushrooms.

4. Bake in the oven for 20-25 minutes at 350F/180C or until mushrooms have cooked and the cheese is nicely melted.

Nutritional info per serving:
Calories: 163kcal, Carbs: 3.29g, Protein: 5.26g, Fat: Dietary Fiber: 0.7g

Cranberry Glazed Turkey Meatballs

A festive meal that is ideal for holiday family or guest parties. The turkey meatballs gain another dimension thanks to the cranberry sauce glaze.

Servings: 30 small meatballs/6 servings

Total cooking time: 35 minutes

Ingredients:

- 1 ¼ pound ground turkey
- 2 large slices wholewheat bread, cut into small cubes
- 1 whole egg
- 2 tbsp milk
- ¼ cup ricotta cheese
- 1 tbsp of dried thyme
- Corn flour (for dusting)
- ⅔ cup sugar-free cranberry sauce
- 3 tbsp of vegetable oil e.g rapeseed oil
- Salt/Pepper

Method:

1. Combine the white bread cubes with the milk and let saturate. Add the egg, thyme, and ricotta cheese. Season with salt/pepper and mix well with your hands.
2. Form around 30 small balls with your hands (a tad smaller than a golf ball)
3. Lightly coat and roll the meatballs in flour and arrange in a large baking sheet with parchment/wax paper.

4. Spray with some cooking spray on top and bake in the oven for 20 minutes at 350F/189C.
5. Heat a medium deep skillet with the vegetable oil over medium heat. Add the meatballs in batches of 8-10 each time. Add one part of the cranberry glaze in each batch and make sure all balls are evenly coated with the cranberry sauce glaze. Leave on the heat for 2 minutes (with the glaze), take off and repeat the same step with the next two batches.
6. Transfer in a big shallow dish and serve warm.

Nutritional info per serving:
Calories: 276kcal, Carbs: 20.3gg, Protein: 22.9g, Fat: 10.6g, Dietary Fiber: 1.6g

Kine Wontons

The Hawaiian version of the well-known Chinese dish of fried wontons made easily with cream cheese and imitation crab meat. Very tasty and great for parties.

Servings: 30 wontons/6 servings

Total cooking time: 12 minutes

Ingredients:

- 8 oz. cream cheese, softened at room temperature
- 5 green onions, chopped
- 2 tbsp soy sauce
- 1 pack (12 oz.) imitation crab meat
- 1 5 oz. can of water chestnuts, washed, drained and finely chopped
- 2 packs (14 oz.) wonton wrappers
- Vegetable oil (for frying)

Method:
1. Combine the cream cheese, green onions, imitation crab meat, soy sauce and water chestnuts in a medium bowl.
2. Place around 1 full tsp of the cream cheese mix in the center of each wonton wrapper. Take the edges and fold each into a triangle, with slightly dampened hands.
3. Heat the oil in a large deep skillet until hot and lightly smoking.
4. Fry the wontons in batches of 10 each time until golden brown.

5. Drain in a large paper towel covered dish and serve hot.

Nutritional info per serving:
Calories: 284kcal, Carbs: 28.6g, Protein: 9.6gg, Fat: 14.9g, Dietary Fiber: 1.6g

Salmon with Creamy Dill Yogurt Sauce

Salmon is one of the richest fish not only in flavor but in good-for your brain omega-3 fatty acids, especially if it's fresh and wild-caught. If you pair it up with a nice creamy yogurt sauce, you have a delicious combo that is full of good fats and other nutrients.

Servings: 2

Total cooking time: 8 minutes

Ingredients:

- 2 fresh, skin-on salmon fillets (for 2 small portions)
- 1 tbsp of fresh dill
- 1 tbsp of lime juice
- 2 tbsp of olive oil
- ½ cup greek yogurt
- 1 tsp of mayo
- ½ tsp garlic powder
- 2 tsp of salt
- ½ tsp black pepper

Method:

1. Season lightly the salmon fillets with 1 tsp of salt and the black pepper. Place on the grill or a pan and cook for around 3 minutes on each side (for medium to well-done results).
2. Combine the yogurt, lime juice, dill, mayo, garlic powder and the rest of the salt in a small bowl.
3. Serve the cooked salmon fillets with the yogurt sauce on the side.

Nutritional info per serving:
Calories: 348kcal, Carbs: 5.1g, Protein: 32.8g,
Fat:21.8g Dietary Fiber: 1.1g

Beef & Pepper Meatloaf

A clean eating meatloaf recipe with the addition of red bell pepper for extra color and flavor. Great for family feasts and as a leftover for sandwiches.

Servings: 8

Total cooking time: 45 minutes

Ingredients:

- 1 ½ pound ground beef (around 90% lean)
- 1 medium red bell pepper, diced
- 1 scallion, chopped
- 1 clove of garlic, minced
- 1 tbsp of mustard
- 1 tsp of paprika
- ⅓ cup oats
- 1 egg white
- 1 tbsp of vegetable oil
- Salt
- Pepper

Method:
4. Heat the oil in a small skillet and add the red bell pepper, scallion, and garlic. Saute for a couple of minutes.
5. In a large bowl, combine the ground beef with the peppers and the rest of the ingredients. Season with salt and pepper to taste.
6. Shape into a meatloaf on a large shallow baking sheet lined with wax paper.
7. Bake in the oven at 350F/180C for 40 minutes.

Nutritional info per serving:
Calories: 251kcal, Carbs: 4.2g, Protein: 16.1g, Fat: 19.1, Dietary Fiber: 1.3g

Curried Cauliflower Rice Salad

A rich and flavorful salad made with cauliflower rice that will keep you feeling full for hours, despite having no meat or protein to support it. A great choice for vegans too.

Servings: 2

Total cooking time: 10 minutes

Ingredients:

- 1 cup of cooked cauliflower rice
- ¼ small red onion, finely chopped
- ½ green bell pepper, diced
- ½ red bell pepper, diced
- 1 stalk of celery
- 1 cup of white cabbage, shredded
- 1 small carrot, peel and shredded

For the dressing:
- 2-3 tbsp balsamic vinegar
- 2-3 tbsp of rice vinegar
- 2 tbsp of mustard
- 2 cloves of garlic, minced
- 1 tsp of light soy sauce
- 2 tsp of curry powder

Method:
1. Combine the cooked cauliflower rice with the diced peppers and the rest of the veggies.
2. In a small dressing bow, combine the ingredients of the dressing and stir well or blend in a food processor.

3. Add the dressing to the rice and vegetable salad and toss.
4. Serve.

Nutritional info per serving:
Calories: 106kcal, Carbs: 9.7g, Protein:2.03g, Fat:0.89g, Dietary Fiber: 1.3g

Stuffed Zucchini

A stuffed zucchini recipe with a lightly cheesy and creamy filling. Great for all seasons and all occasions.

Servings: 4

Total cooking time: 30 minutes

Ingredients:

- 2 medium zucchini
- ½ small white onion, chopped
- 1 egg, lightly beaten
- ¼ cup dry breadcrumbs
- ¼ cup grated parmesan cheese
- 1 tbsp of parsley, finely chopped
- 1 tbsp of cooking oil

Method:

1. Cut zucchini in half, lengthwise.
2. Scoop out with a spoon or ice cream scooper and reserve the pulp, leaving out an approx. 1/3 inch thick shell. Cut the pulp into extra small chunks.
3. Heat oil in a pan over medium heat and add the onion and zucchini pulp. Saute until tender.
4. Remove from heat and combine with the rest of the ingredients. Fill the zucchini shells with the mixture. Place in a baking sheet lined with wax paper.
5. Bake for 20-25 minutes at 350F/180C.

Nutritional info per serving:
Calories: 211kcal, Carbs: 16.8g, Protein:9.04g, Dietary Fiber: 3.3g

Pad Kee Mao

Pad Kee Mao is a classic Thai dish that essentially means "drunken noodles" as it features a 4-sauce marinade and a bit of wine to make. Very delicious and perfect for vegans too.

Servings: 4

Total cooking time: 15 minutes.

Ingredients:

- 8 oz. cooked rice noodles
- 2 shallots, diced
- 1 scallion, julienned
- 4 Thai red chili peppers, deseeded and sliced
- 1 cup holy basil leaves, washed and drained
- 6 pieces of baby corn, cut in half lengthwise
- 3 tbsp of light soy sauce
- 2 tsp of oyster sauce
- 1 tbsp fish sauce
- 1 ½ tsp brown sugar
- 3 cloves of garlic, minced
- 2 tbsp of white wine
- 3 tbsp of canola oil

Method:
1. Heat the oil over medium heat in a wok until it's lightly smoking and saute the garlic and ginger first for a minute so they release their natural aromas. Add the scallions and the shallot and saute for another minute.

2. In a small bowl, combine all the liquid sauces e.g soy sauce with the sugar and wine.
3. Add the baby corns, holy basil, and the peppers to the wok and stir. Add the rice noodles, stir well, and top with the prepared soy sauce mixture. Stir with a flat spatula and make sure the sauce covers everything.
4. Serve warm.

Nutritional info per serving:
Calories: 237kcal, Carbs: 27.1g, Protein: 3.7g, Fat:13.1g, Dietary Fiber: 2.1g

Tuna Dip

A creamy tuna dip made with tuna in a jar, cream cheese and a mild mix of herbs. Great with tortilla corn chips.

Servings: 6

Total cooking time: 3 minutes of prep.

Ingredients:

- 1 jar of tuna (around 100 grams), drained
- 1 cup cream cheese, softened at room temperature
- 1 tsp prepared horseradish
- ½ cup sour cream
- 1 tsp Worcestershire sauce
- 2 tbsp onion, finely chopped
- ½ clove of garlic

Method:

1. Combine the Worcestershire with the horseradish sauce and add the cream cheese, onion, and garlic.
2. Add in the sour cream and stir well.
3. Add the tuna and mix again with a fork or spatula.
4. Serve with some dips of your choice e.g pitta chips or corn tortilla chips.

Nutritional info per serving:
Calories: 192kcal, Carbs: 3.4g, Protein: 13.7g, Fat:13.9g, Dietary Fiber:0.4g

Veal Goulash

A melt-in-your-mouth Goulash recipe with veal, probiotic-rich sauerkraut as a side, spices and cultured sour cream.

Servings: 8

Total cooking time: 1 ½ hour

Ingredients:

- 2 pounds of veal, cut into big cubes
- 1 ½ cup of sliced white onions
- 1 tsp garlic, minced
- 1 cup tomato puree
- 1 cup full-fat sour cream
- 4 tbsp unsalted butter
- 2 tsp caraway seeds
- 2 30 oz. jars sauerkraut
- 2 tsp paprika powder
- 3 tbsp fresh parsley, chopped
- 2 cups of water
- Salt
- Pepper

Method:
1. Heat the butter in a deep pan over medium heat and lightly brown the veal. Work in batches of 2-3. Season with the salt.
2. Return all veal cubes to the pan and add the onions and garlic. Cook for another 3 minutes.
3. Add salt and pepper to taste and add the tomatoes. Add around 2 cups of water to cover the veal mixture.

4. Lower the heat and simmer for around 30 minutes uncovered. After 30 minutes have passed, remove the veal from the pan and reduce the sauce by increasing heat and let the sauce boil for 7-8 minutes.
5. Return the veal cubes to the pan and add the paprika and sour cream. Let simmer uncovered for another 30 minutes.
6. Add last the caraway seeds, toss and finish off with the parsley.
7. Serve with sauerkraut on the side.

Nutritional info per serving:
Calories: 285kcal, Carbs: 10.2g, Protein: 25.2g, Fat:16.2g, Dietary Fiber: 5.2g

Dinner recipes

Lemon Chicken & Spinach

A comforting dish with lemon, chicken, and spinach that is something between a stew and soup in texture. This dish is full of protein, vitamins A, C, E, K, phosphorus, and potassium.

Servings: 2

Total Cooking Time: 30 minutes

Ingredients:

- 2 large, skin-off chicken breasts
- 2 cups of fresh spinach, roughly chopped
- 1 small red onion, thinly chopped
- 2 cups of chicken-vegetable stock
- 2 tbsp of lemon juice
- ½ tsp nutmeg
- 1 tbsp sour cream
- 1 tbsp butter
- Pepper

Method:
1. Heat the butter in a skillet and add the onion. Cook until transparent (around 2 minutes). Add the spinach and cook to wilt for another 2 minutes. Season the nutmeg and pepper.
2. Add the whole chicken breast and cook halfway through for around 3 minutes. Add the lemon and chicken stock and reduce the heat. Simmer everything for 20 minutes.

3. Add the sour cream towards the last minute and stir to incorporate.
4. Serve warm.

Nutritional info per serving:
Calories: 572kcal, Carbs: 19.1g, Protein: 83.9g, Fat:17.1, Dietary Fiber:2.6g.

Roasted Red Pepper Soup

A delicious red pepper soup that resembles pizza in aromas and flavors, thanks to the roasting process and the addition of herbs. Great for an autumn or winter dinner.

Servings: 6

Total cooking time:40 minutes

Ingredients:

- 6-7 red bell peppers, washed and deseeded
- ½ white onion chopped
- 3 tbsp olive oil
- 5 cloves of garlic, smashed
- 4 cups chicken stock
- 2 tsp hot sauce
- ½ tsp salt
- ¼ cup sour cream
- 1 tsp dried oregano

Method:

1. Cut and deseed the peppers in half (lengthwise) and arrange in a baking sheet covered with parchment paper. Place the smashed garlic in between the peppers and drizzle with 2 tsp of olive oil.
2. Place in your oven's broiler for 15 minutes. Remove from the oven and place in a glass or plastic container with the lid on to trap the heat and steam and soften up the bell peppers.

3. While the peppers are prepared, saute the onions with the rest of the olive oil until soft and translucent.
4. Peel off the burned skin from the roasted and softened peppers.
5. Place the roasted peppers, garlic and onions in a food processor until smooth and no large chunks are left.
6. Add the pepper mixture into a large saucepan or pot with the chicken stock, hot sauce, and salt. Let it simmer for 15 minutes and add the sour cream last. Stir.
7. Sprinkle the oregano on top and serve warm.

Nutritional info per serving:
Calories: 129kcal, Carbs: 12.3g, Protein: 1.9g, Fat:8.1g, Dietary Fiber:3g.

Salmon Mousse

A very rich and creamy salmon mousse that is perfect for guest dinner parties.

Servings: 12

Total cooking time: 8 minutes of prep.

Ingredients:

- 1lb of boneless steamed salmon, chopped
- ¼ cup onion, finely chopped
- ½ cup diced celery
- ½ cup green bell pepper, diced
- 2 tbsp fresh dill, chopped
- ½ cup plain yogurt
- ½ cup mayonnaise
- 1 pack (8 oz. cream cheese)
- 1 tsp tabasco sauce
- 3 tbsp lemon juice
- ¾ cup of cold water
- 4 tsp plain gelatin

Method:
1. Mix the salmon, celery, green pepper, onion, dill, mayonnaise, tabasco, yogurt, lemon juice in a bowl.
2. Soften the cream cheese in a saucepan over medium heat for a minute and then add to the salmon mixture.
3. Dissolve the gelatin in a separate bowl with the cold water and stir well.
4. Add the gelatin to the dissolved mixture and stir well.

5. Place into a decorative silicon mold or 12 small individual serving balls and refrigerate for at least 5-6 hours.
6. To release the mouse from the mold more easily, place the base in hot water, shake for a few seconds, and gently slide off the mold.
7. Serve in an oblong dish.

Nutritional info per serving:
Calories: 204kcal, Carbs: 2.79g, Protein: 11.8g, Fat:16.1g, Dietary Fiber:0.4g

Sundried Tomato & Stuffed Artichoke

A hearty artichoke recipe inspired by Mediterranean flavors that is great for large families or guest parties. If you are allergic to mushrooms you may substitute this with artichokes

Servings: 8 artichokes

Total cooking time: 25-30 minutes

Ingredients:

- 8 medium artichoke hearts, from a frozen pack
- ½ oz. sun-dried tomatoes (about 5 pieces), chopped finely
- ½ cup shallots, finely chopped
- ⅓ cup dry breadcrumbs
- 2 garlic cloves, minced
- 1 large egg, beaten lightly
- ¼ cup fresh parsley leaves washed well and cut
- ½ tsp dried basil
- 2 tbsp ground parmesan
- ⅓ cup cheddar cheese
- 3 tbsp olive oil
- Salt/Pepper

Method:
1.Preheat the oven at 400F/190C.
2. Pre-boil the artichoke hearts to soften in 4 cups of water for 8 minutes,
3. While the artichokes cook, heat 2 tbsp of olive oil in a skillet, and add the shallots and garlic, stirring occasionally until shallots have softened.

4. Combine in a bowl the cooked shallots, garlic, breadcrumbs, sun-dried tomatoes, egg, parsley, basil, salt and pepper to taste.

5. Spoon the stuffing in the artichoke caps and arrange on a baking sheet lined with parchment paper.

6. Sprinkle with the parmesan and cheddar cheese on top and bake in the oven for 15 minutes (at 375F/189C).

Nutritional info per serving:
Calories: 167kcal, Carbs: 20.1g, Protein: 6.3g, Fat: 8.2g, Dietary Fiber: 0.5g

Feta Saganaki

A Greek treat typically served in Greek Tavernas as a mezze dish that bursts with Mediterranean flavors of feta, black olives, and oregano.

Servings: 4

Total cooking time: 16 minutes

Ingredients:

- 1 block (8 oz.) feta cheese, liquids drained
- 4 cherry tomatoes, halved
- ⅓ cup black kalamata olives pitted
- 1 medium red onion, sliced
- 1 tsp of oregano
- A drizzle of olive oil

Method:
1. Cut the block of feta cheese in 4 equal parts.
2. Transfer in a square sheet of aluminum foil lined with parchment paper(around 8X4") drizzle with olive oil and arrange the rest of the ingredients on top and to the sides. Sprinkle the oregano on top.
3. Fold the aluminum foil and parchment paper from the 4 sides to make a packet, leaving a bit of the fetta mixture exposed in the middle.
4. Bake in the oven for 15 minutes at 375F/175F.

Nutritional info per serving:
Calories: 196kcal, Carbs:4.04g, Protein: 8.35g, Fat: 16.6g, Dietary Fiber: 0.7g

Asparagus, Goat cheese & Lemon Cauliflower Rice

A unique cauliflower rice combination for lovers of goat cheese and asparagus. If you are fed up with ordinary tomato or cheesy pasta, this is a great recipe to go for.

Servings: 6

Total cooking time: 15 minutes

Ingredients:

- 3 cups of cauliflower rice
- 1 pound thin asparagus spears, trimmed and chopped to 1" long pieces
- 1 5 oz. pack soft goat cheese
- 2 tsp saffron (optional)
- 1 tsp lemon zest
- Fresh lemon juice (to taste)
- ¼ cup olive oil
- 1 tsp salt

Method:

1. Cook the cauliflower rice according to package instructions. Add the asparagus pieces and cook for another 3 minutes. Drain and keep aside.
2. Combine in a large salad bowl the olive oil, lemon juice, and goat cheese. Stir well.
3. Add the cooked pasta and asparagus to the mix and stir well to combine everything.
4. Serve with some saffron leaves on top (optional) for garnishing.

Nutritional info per serving:
Calories:184kcal, Carbs: 6.4g, Protein: 7.2g, Fat: 15.5g,
Dietary Fiber: 2.5g

Spicy Lamb Balls

A lovely recipe with ground lamb and several spices that give it that extra kick of flavor. These are totally awesome served with pitta bread and some tzatziki sauce.

Servings: 6 (around 12-14 balls)

Total cooking time:25 minutes

Ingredients:

- 1 lb ground lamb
- 1 small onion, grated
- 1 egg white
- ½ cup of breadcrumbs
- 2 cloves of garlic, minced
- ¼ cup fresh coriander, finely chopped
- 1 tsp of cumin
- 1 tsp of paprika
- ½ tsp of dry coriander
- ½ tsp cinnamon
- ½ tsp salt
- 1 tbsp of olive oil

Method:
1. Combine all the ingredients except for the oil in a mixing bowl.
2. Shape into small meatballs with your hands. Flatten slightly with your hands (they should look something between a ball and a patty).
3. Grease a grilling skillet with the olive oil. Add the balls in 2 batches of 6-7 balls each time and cook for

approx. 3 minutes on each side. (for a medium to well-done result).
4. Serve warm.

Nutritional info per serving:
Calories: 214kcal, Carbs: 8.5g, Protein:17.2g, Fat:12.2, Dietary Fiber:1g

Grilled Oysters

A simple yet delicious way to enjoy oysters (if you don't like the thought of eating them raw with some lemon juice). The recipe is full of zinc, phosphorus and

Servings: 5   (15 oysters)

Total cooking time: 15 minutes

Ingredients:

- 15 whole live oysters
- 3 tbsp unsalted butter
- 2 cloves of garlic, minced
- 1 tsp of lemon juice
- ½ tsp red chili flakes
- ¼ tsp salt
- 1 tbsp parsley leaves, finely chopped
- 3 tbsp olive oil

Method:

1. To make your sauce, heat a small pan over medium heat and add the butter and the olive oil. Add the garlic and saute until fragrant. Add lemon juice, pepper chili flakes, salt, and parsley. Stir well.
2. Turn off the heat. Place the oysters (cap facing up) on a hot grill surface, cover and cook for a minute. The oysters should open lightly at this point.
3. Remove from the heat and take a screw or shucking knife to open the oyster more.
4. Spoon a bit of the sauce over each oyster and return to the grill. Cover the lid of the surface and cook for another 4-5 minutes.

Nutritional info per serving:
Calories: 238kcal, Carbs: 8.1gg, Protein: 5.8g, Fat: 16.2, Dietary Fiber:0.3g.

Broccoli & Garlic Roast

A tasty dinner side made with broccoli, garlic and a light cheesy touch of parmesan cheese.

Servings: 6

Total cooking time: 10 minutes

Ingredients:

- 3 cups of broccoli florets
- 5 cloves of garlic, minced
- ½ tsp chili flakes
- 2 tbsp olive oil
- 2 tbsp parmesan cheese
- 3 cups of water
- 1 tsp salt

Method:

1. Cook the broccoli for approx. 8 minutes in a pot filled with water and salt.
2. Meanwhile, heat the olive oil in a small pan and add the minced garlic. Saute over medium heat for 1 minute or until fragrant. Add the chili flakes and cook for another minute or so.
3. Drain the broccoli pieces and place them in a deep serving dish. Add the garlic and pepper flake mixture on top and stir to spread and even out the ingredients.
4. Top with the parmesan cheese and serve.

Nutritional info per serving:
Calories:61kcal, Carbs: 3g, Protein: 1.7g, Fat:5.1g, Dietary Fiber:0.9g

Italian Sausage, Peppers & Arugula Salad

A very easy recipe that combines the rich flavors of peppers and Italian pork sausages with a hint of sweetness from the balsamic and honey vinaigrette

Servings: 6

Total cooking time: 5 minutes

Ingredients:

- 1 pound of Italian sausage links, cut into large 2-3" pieces
- 1 large white onion, sliced
- 1 large red bell pepper, cut into large squares
- 2 tbsp of honey
- 2 tbsp of balsamic vinegar
- 2 cups of baby arugula leaves, roughly chopped

Method:

1. Heat the olive oil in a skillet and add the onions, peppers, and sausage. Saute for 3-4 minutes.
2. Combine in a small bowl the honey and balsamic vinegar to make your dressing.
3. Arrange the arugula leaves on a deep yet long serving dish and add the dressing, giving it a light toss to distribute.
4. Place and spread the pepper and sausage mixture on top of the arugula leaves.
5. Serve.

Nutritional info per serving:

Calories:154kcal, Carbs:11.6g, Protein:12.9g,Fat: 6.4g,
Dietary Fiber:0.7g

Green Pea Soup

A lovely green pea soup that is incredibly delicious and healthy at the same time. This great for vegans too as it has no animal ingredients whatsoever.

Servings:6

Total cooking time: 25 minutes

Ingredients:

- 3 ½ cups frozen peas
- 3 cups of vegetable broth
- 2 serrano chilies, stemmed and chopped
- 6 cloves of garlic, minced
- 1 medium white onion, chopped
- 3 tbsp sunflower oil
- 3 tbsp of fresh ginger, grated
- 1 tsp salt

Method:

1. Heat the sunflower oil in a pot and add the white onion. Saute until transparent (around 2-3 minutes) and add the garlic and the ginger. Add the serrano chilies and saute for another couple of minutes.
2. Add the frozen peas, give everything a good stir and add the vegetable broth, Bring to a boil and let cook until peas have softened up (around 15 minutes).
3. Transfer the mixture into a food processor or use an immersion blender directly on the pot to blend the mixture into a creamy green soup.
4. Season with the salt and serve hot.

Nutritional info per serving:
Calories:118kcal, Carbs:10.9g, Protein:2.8g, Fat:7.3g,
Dietary Fiber: 3.2g

Grilled Paprika Shrimp Skewers

A lovely shrimp recipe for the barbeque or grill pan that bursts with the flavors of paprika and lime juice.

Servings: 4

Total prep & cooking time: 1 hour

Ingredients:

- 1 lb. large shrimps, cleaned, peeled and deveined
- ⅓ cup olive oil
- 2 cloves of garlic, minced
- 1 tbsp of sweet paprika
- 2 tbsp of smoked paprika
- 2 tbsp lime juice
- ½ tsp cayenne pepper
- 1/2 tsp salt
- ½ tsp freshly ground pepper
- 4-5 bamboo skewers

Method:

1. Combine all the ingredients except for the shrimps in a bowl to make your marinade.
2. Place the shrimps in the marinade and let marinate for at least 40 minutes in the fridge. Keep the marinade aside
3. Heat a grilling surface. Pass the marinated shrimps through 4-5 bamboo skewers (around 3 shrimps in each).
4. Cook the shrimp skewers for a couple of minutes on each side. Use a brush to occasionally brush the remaining marinade on the shrimps while they cook.

5. Serve warm.

Nutritional info per serving:
Calories: 258kcal, Carbs: 5.2g, Protein: 16.3g,
Fat:19.6g, Dietary Fiber: 2g

Creamy Polenta & Mushrooms

A restaurant-quality recipe that is great for any occasion and thanks to the hearty "drunk" mushrooms and the creamy polenta combo, this will keep you satiated without any meat or protein necessary.

Servings: 4

Total cooking time: 15 minutes

Ingredients:

- 1 cup polenta/cornmeal mush powder
- 4 small white mushrooms, stems trimmed and thickly sliced
- ⅓ cup red wine
- 1 clove of garlic, minced
- 1 small sweet onion, sliced
- 1 cup vegetable broth
- ⅔ cup milk
- 2 tbsp parmesan cheese
- 3 tbsp sunflower oil
- ½ tsp salt
- ½ tsp pepper

Method:
1. Heat the oil in a pan and add the sliced mushrooms with the onion. Saute until softened and until most of the liquid has evaporated (around 5 minutes) over medium heat. Add the garlic and saute for another minute.
2. Add the wine to the pan, toss and cook until the wine has evaporated. Remove from the heat and

keep the mushroom mixture aside. Season with salt and pepper.

3. In a deep saucepan, prepare the polenta with half of the vegetable broth and the milk. Bring to a simmer and stir occasionally until nearly all the liquid has evaporated. Add the remaining stock in 2-3 parts to prevent any lumps.
4. Once you get too creamy/mushy consistency to add the parmesan cheese, stir and remove from the heat.
5. To serve, add one part of polenta (around 4 tbsp) in a deep dish and one part of the mushroom mixture on top. Make sure all 4 portions are equally distributed.

Nutritional info per serving:
Calories:202kcal, Carbs:18.11g, Protein:4.06g, Fat:,
Dietary Fiber: 1.2g

Indian Curry Chickpeas

A comforting Indian recipe that is bursting with spices and aromas. The recipe is so rich and filling that you won't miss meat if you are a vegan.

Servings: 2

Ingredients:

- 1 cup of chickpeas, cooked
- 1 onion chopped
- 1 tomato, chopped
- 1 tsp garam masala
- 1 tsp turmeric
- 3 tbsp olive oil
- 4 cloves garlic, minced
- 1 green chili pepper
- 1 piece fresh ginger
- 2 bay leaves
- 3 tbsp olive oil
- 2 cups of water
- Salt
- Pepper

Method:

1. Grind the tomato, onion, garlic and chili pepper in the food processor until you make a paste.
2. Heat the olive oil in a deep skillet over medium heat. Saute the bay leaves for 1 minute or until fragrant.
3. Pour the tomato paste and stir for a few seconds. Add the fresh ginger, garam masala, turmeric,

salt, and pepper. Cook for another 3 minutes.
4. Add the cooked chickpeas and the water to cover. Reduce the heat and bring to a boil. Remove from the heat.
5. Serve warm.

Nutritional info per serving:
Calories:413kcal, Carbs:46.2g, Protein:9.4g, Fat:22.8g, Dietary Fiber: 9.9g

Liver Pate

An incredibly rich French pate recipe made with meat and liver and amplified by a unique blend of spices for extra flavor. This recipe is incredibly rich in B-complex vitamins, Omega-3 fatty acids, iron, and selenium.

Servings: 10

Total Cooking Time: 1 hour & 40 minutes

Ingredients:

- 1 lb lean ground pork
- 1 lb chicken liver, extra fat and connective tissue removed, diced
- ½ small onion
- ¼ tsp ginger powder
- '¼ tsp clove
- ⅓ tsp nutmeg
- 1 clove of garlic
- 1 tbsp cognac or brandy
- 1 tbsp dry sherry wine
- 2 sprigs of parsley
- Dash of tabasco sauce
- ½ lb sliced bacon
- Salt

Method:

1. Process the diced liver, sherry, cognac, onion, garlic, ginger, parsley and spices in a food processor. Season with salt and a dash of tabasco sauce.

2. Mix with the ground pork.
3. Arrange a terrine or long cake dish with the strips of bacon covering all sides. Make sure the top side is covered with bacon slices as well.
4. Place hot water in a large baking dish to make a water bath and place the terrine dish with the liver pork mixture on top.
5. Cook uncovered at 350/175C for 90 minutes.
6. Remove from the oven and let rest at room temperature for 15 minutes.
7. Place in the fridge for at least 6 hours before serving.
8. Serve sliced with French bread and white or rose wine.

Nutritional info per serving:
Calories:182kcal, Carbs:0g, Protein:25.4g, Fat: 8.1g, Dietary Fiber: 0g

Lentils & Spinach Stew

This hearty stew recipe with lentils and spinach is perfect for autumn and winter. This combo is not only delicious, but it is also rich in iron, vitamin A, and vitamin K.

Servings: 4

Total Cooking Time: 1 hour

Ingredients:

- 1 (10.oz) pack frozen spinach
- ½ cup lentils
- 2 white onions
- 1 tsp ground cumin
- 2 cloves garlic, minced
- 1 tbsp vegetable oil
- 2 cups of water
- Salt
- Pepper

Method:

1. Heat the oil in a skillet over medium heat. Add the onions and saute for around 8 minutes. Add the garlic and saute until fragrant for one minute.
2. Add the lentils and water to the saucepan. Bring to a boil. Cover and let simmer for 35 minutes.
3. Add the spinach to the lentil mixture and add salt and cumin. Cook for another 10 minutes.
4. Season optionally with salt and pepper to taste.

Nutritional info per serving:
Calories:165kcal, Carbs:24g, Protein:9.7g, Fat: 4.3g,
Dietary Fiber: 10.4g

Cauliflower Soup with Turmeric & Ginger

This soup recipe is ideally seasoned with the rich and zingy flavors and aromas of turmeric and ginger. A superfood soup recipe that you don't want to miss.

Servings: 4

Total Cooking Time: 20 minutes

Ingredients:

- 2 cups cauliflower florets
- 4 cups of vegetable broth
- 2 shallot, chopped
- 1 tsp turmeric powder
- 1 tbsp fresh ginger, minced
- 2 tbsp butter
- 2 tbsp of heavy cream
- Salt
- Pepper

Method:

5. Add the cauliflower to boil in 4 cups of vegetable broth. Bring to a boil and cook covered for 15 minutes.
6. Meanwhile, heat the butter in a skillet and add the shallots, ginger and turmeric powder. Cook until fragrant for 2 minutes.
7. Process the boiled cauliflower with the spicy shallot mixture and the heavy cream in a food processor until creamy and smooth. Season with salt and pepper to taste.

8. Serve warm.

Nutritional info per serving:
Calories:117kcal, Carbs:9.2g, Protein:2.11g, Fat: 8.7g,
Dietary Fiber: 3g

Dessert recipes

3-ingredient Brownies

It may sound unbelievable but you can actually make healthy and delicious brownies with just 3 ingredients. These are so easy that even a kid can make them.

Servings: 15

Total Cooking Time: 25 minutes

Ingredients:

- ⅓ cup almond butter (no salt)
- ¼ cup unsweetened cocoa powder
- 3 ripe bananas

Method:
1. Preheat the oven at 350F/180C.
2. Blend everything in a food processor until smooth.
3. Arrange in a non-stick and lightly greased baking dish. Bake for 20 minutes.
4. Let rest for 10 minutes and cut into around 2X3" squares with a sharp knife. You may also refrigerate for around 1 hour before serving.

Nutritional info per serving:
Calories: 285kcal, Carbs:15.6g, Protein:9.3g, Fat: 23.4g, Dietary Fiber:5.6g

Hearty Oat Cookies

A super easy, healthy and delicious recipe made with oats and raisins. The texture is also something between chewy and crunchy so if you like your cookies in-between, this is perfect.

Servings: 20 cookies

Total Cooking Time: 20 minutes

Ingredients:
- 1 ripe banana
- ½ cup apple sauce
- 4 tbsp agave syrup
- 2 cups rolled oats
- ½ cup raisins

Method:
1. Preheat the oven at 380F/190C.
2. Mash the ripe banana in a bowl and then add the applesauce and agave syrup and stir.
3. Add in the rolled oats and raisins and stir well.
4. Scoop the cookie dough with an ice-cream scooper to make 20 small cookies on a baking dish lined with parchment paper.
5. Bake the cookies until golden brown for 15-20 minutes.
6. Once baked, transfer to a cooling rack and let cool for 10 minutes.
7. Serve. You may keep this for up to 5 days in a cookie jar at room temperature.

Nutritional info per serving:
Calories:62kcal, Carbs:13.5g, Protein:1.3g, Fat:0.6g ,
Dietary Fiber:1.2g

Pomegranate Yogurt Dessert

A decadent yet refreshing dessert made with Greek yogurt and the antioxidant-rich pomegranate. Ready in just 3 minutes.

Servings: 4

Total Cooking Time: 3 minutes

Ingredients:

- 2 cups Greek Yogurt
- ½ tsp orange blossom water
- 2 tbsp honey
- 1 large pomegranate, seeds removed
- A few small mint leaves (for garnishing)

Method:
1. Combine the Greek yogurt with the honey and orange blossom water.
2. Distribute the mixture into 4 medium-sized mason jars and sprinkle the pomegranate seeds on top. Garnish each jar with 1-2 mint leaves

Nutritional info per serving:
Calories: 262kcal, Carbs:38g, Protein:8.1g, Fat: 8g, Dietary Fibre:4g

Avocado Ice Cream

An incredibly rich and creamy ice-cream recipe with healthy avocado and coconut fats.

Ingredients:

- 1 14.oz full fat coconut cream
- 2 ripe avocados, peeled and pitted
- 1 ripe banana
- 3 tbsp maple syrup
- 2 tbsp lime juice
- A few mint leaves, for garnishing

Method:

1. Chill a long loaf pan in the fridge for 2 hours.
2. Process the avocados, banana, coconut cream and lime juice in a food processor until creamy and smooth.
3. Transfer the mixture into a chilled loaf pan and use a spoon's backside to even the mixture out.
4. Chill in the freezer for at least 5 hours before serving. Garnish optionally with a few mint leaves.

Nutritional info per serving:

Calories: 293kcal, Carbs:19.1g, Protein:3g, Fat: 15.2g, Dietary Fiber:5g

Blueberry Smoothie Popsicles

A refreshing summer treat that is very kid and family-friendly as the mixture is made into cute popsicles. Very rich in probiotics and antioxidants

Servings: 4

Total Cooking Time: 2 minutes prep.

Ingredients:

- 2 (5.3 oz.) containers of Greek Vanilla-flavor yogurt
- ⅓ cup of frozen blueberries
- 1 tbsp of agave syrup
- 1 tsp lemon zest

Method:
1. Blend everything together in a blender until creamy and smooth.
2. Transfer the yogurt mixture into 4 small-sized popsicle molds.
3. Place in the freezer for at least 6 hours before serving.

Nutritional info per serving:
Calories:76kcal, Carbs:11.9g, Protein:6.8g, Fat:0.2g, Dietary Fiber:0.6g

Frozen Banana Yogurt Bites

Another tasty frozen treat with banana, yogurt and chocolate chips. Very family-friendly and easy to make.

Total Cooking Time: **10 minutes prep.**

Ingredients:

- 1 large ripe banana
- 150g. Greek yogurt
- 12 banana chips

Method:

1. Mash the banana with a fork and combine it with the Greek yogurt.
2. Transfer the mixture into 12 small cupcake cases or silicone molds. Arrange one banana chip on top of each bite.
3. Place over a flat baking sheet and transfer the bites to the freezer. Let in the freeze for at least 6 hours before serving.

Nutritional info per serving:
Calories: 61kcal, Carbs: 7.9g, Protein:1.5g, Fat:2.8g, Dietary Fiber:0.9g

Apple & Spice Cake

A must-try cake recipe bursting with the Autumn flavors of apples and spices.

Servings: 1 cake/12 serving

Total Cooking Time: 25 minutes

Ingredients:

- 1 cup of unsweetened applesauce
- 1 ½ cups of oats
- 2 scoops of protein powder
- 2 tbsp unsweetened almond milk
- 2 tbsp stevia
- 2 tbsp maple syrup
- 3 egg whites
- 1 tsp cinnamon
- ½ tsp nutmeg
- ½ tsp baking soda

Method:
1. Add everything in a food processor and blend until creamy and smooth.
2. Transfer the mixture into a lightly greased 8X8" baking sheet.
3. Bake in the oven at 350F/180C for 25 minutes.

Nutritional info per serving:
Calories: 105kcal, Carbs:15g, Protein:8g, Fat:1.2g , Dietary Fiber: 1.5g

Baked Peaches with Ricotta Cheese

A hearty recipe made with roasted peaches and ricotta cheese. An impressive guest hit for sure.

Servings: 4

Total Cooking Time: 6-8 minutes

Ingredients:

- 4 just-ripe medium peaches, pitted and halved
- 1 cup (200grams) ricotta cheese
- ½ tsp cinnamon
- 1 tbsp of honey

Method:

1. Preheat oven's grill on medium to high heat.
2. Line a baking sheet with parchment paper and arrange the peaches on top.
3. Spoon the ricotta cheese onto the halves and sprinkle with cinnamon.
4. Grill the peaches with the ricotta cheese for 6 minutes.
5. Drizzle a bit of honey and serve.

Nutritional info per serving:
Calories: 180kcal, Carbs:22g, Protein:8g, Fat: 5g, Dietary Fiber: 3.9g

Cocoa & Coconut Chia Pudding

A decadent recipe with omega-3 enriched chia seeds and antioxidant cocoa. This is an overnight recipe that you can enjoy the next morning.

Servings: 5

Ingredients:

- 1 1/2 cup unsweetened almond milk
- ¼ cup cocoa powder sifted
- ½ tsp cinnamon
- 1 pinch sea salt
- ½ tsp vanilla extract
- 3 tbsp maple syrup
- ½ cup chia seeds

Method:

1. Combine the cocoa with the vanilla extract, cinnamon, maple syrup, and salt.
2. Add the almond milk to the cocoa mixture (little at a time) and stir well.
3. Add the chia seeds and mix with a spoon.
4. Transfer into 4 small mason jars and let chill overnight or for at least 6 hours.

Nutritional info per serving:
Calories:172kcal, Carbs:22.1g, Protein:4.7g, Fat:7.8g, Dietary Fiber:8.3g

Blueberry Soup

A cold dessert soup with blueberry and honeydew melon. Perfect for warm summer months.

Servings: 6

Total Cooking Time: 5 minutes prep

Ingredients:

- 1 honeydew melon, peeled, seeded and cubed
- 1 pint of blueberries
- 6 oatmeal cookies, crumbled

Method:

1. Pulse the melon chunks in the food processor. Distribute the mixture on to 6 medium mason jars.
2. Place the blueberries on top and add the oatmeal cookie crumble on top of each serving.
3. Serve chilled.

Nutritional info per serving:
Calories:176kcal, Carbs:25.g, Protein:2.5g, Fat:0g, Dietary Fiber:3.4g

Homemade Hot Fudge

A vegan-friendly hot fudge recipe made with healthy vegetable oils, cocoa, and cashew butter.

Servings: 6

Total Cooking Time: 8 minutes

Ingredients:

- 6 tbsp cashew butter
- 6 tbsp cocoa butter
- 2 tbsp coconut oil
- 2 tbsp walnut oil
- ½ tsp vanilla
- ½ tsp sea salt

Method:

1. Add the oils in a saucepan to melt, over medium heat.
2. Add in the cashew butter and stir well.
3. Add the remaining ingredients except for salt and vanilla and stir.
4. Take off the heat and add vanilla and salt.

Nutritional info per serving:
Calories:209kcal, Carbs:12g, Protein:4g, Fat:6g , Dietary Fiber:2g

Mexican Mango

A delicious recipe made with mango, chili and a hint of lemon. Very easy to make and can be served alone or as a topping for other cream-based desserts.

Servings: 2

Total Cooking Time: 10 minutes

Ingredients:

- 1 large mango, peeled and sliced
- 3 tbsp lemon juice
- 1 tbsp chili powder
- ¼ cup of water
- ½ tsp salt

Method:

1. Add the water into a small saucepan and bring to a boil. Add the lemon juice, salt, and chili powder and whisk well.
2. Add the sliced mango and toss well to coat with the water mixture. Allow the mango to soak in the sauce for a few minutes before serving.

Nutritional Info Per Serving:
Calories:85kcal, Carbs:21.7g, Protein:1.1g, Fat: 0g, Dietary Fiber:3.3g

Almond Flour Cake With Figs

A delicious gluten-free cake made with almond flour and figs. The meringue frosting adds another dimension to the dish.

Servings: 12

Total Cooking Time: 1 hour

Ingredients:

- 2 cups almond flour
- ¼ cup arrowroot powder
- ¾ tsp baking powder
- 34 tsp soda
- 5 eggs, whites, and yolks separated
- ½ cup of honey
- ½ cup of coconut oil
- 2 tbsp almond milk
- 3 tbsp orange zest
- 1 tsp almond extract
- 1 tsp salt

For the meringue frosting
- 4 egg whites
- ⅓ cup honey

Method:
1. Preheat the oven to 300F/148C
2. Use the coconut oil to grease the 2 6" cake/loaf pans. Dust with a little the arrowroot powder.
3. Mix the almond flour, arrowroot, soda, baking powder, and salt.

4. In a separate bowl, mix together the egg yolks, almond milk, coconut oil, honey, and orange zest.
5. Beat the egg whites until solid and stiff.
6. Add the egg yolk mixture to the dry ingredient mix and mix well until no flour is left.
7. Slowly incorporate the egg whites and chopped figs until they are well incorporated into the mixture.
8. Pour the cake batter onto the greased cake pans. Let bake for 50 minutes.
9. Meanwhile, prepare your meringue frosting: Fill a saucepan with a few inches of water and bring to a boil. Add the egg whites and honey to a heatproof bowl and place over the saucepan with the water. Beat the eggs and honey constantly for 5-7 minutes. Bring to a temperature of 140F.
10. Remove the egg whites from the heat and blend with an immersion blender to make it fluffy and smooth.
11. Once the cake is baked, apply the frosting on top with a spatula. Serve.

Nutritional Info Per Serving:
Calories:216kcal, Carbs:26g, Protein:6g, Fat:1g ,
Dietary Fiber:3.1g

Avocado Chocolate Pudding

A superfood chocolate pudding recipe that is packed with healthy fats, iron, and Vitamin A. Ready in just 2 minutes.

Servings: 4

Total Cooking Time: 2 minutes

Ingredients:

- 2 large avocados, peeled and pitted
- ½ cup unsweetened cocoa powder
- ½ cup brown sugar
- ⅓ cup of coconut milk
- 2 tbsp vanilla extract
- 1 pinch ground cinnamon

Method:
1. Blend all the ingredients in a blender until smooth and creamy.
2. Transfer into a large glass bowl and chill in the fridge for at least 1 hour before serving.

Nutritional Info Per Serving:
Calories:400kcal, Carbs:45.9g, Protein:5.4g, Fat:26.3g , Dietary Fiber:13.4g

Cherry Coconut Sorbet

A totally refreshing and cool treat made with just 3 ingredients. No churning or ice-cream maker needed.

Servings: 4

Total Cooking Time: 3 minutes prep

Ingredients:
.

- 2 cups of frozen cherries, pitted
- 2 frozen bananas, peeled
- 1 cup of coconut milk

Method:
1. Add everything into a food processor and process until creamy and smooth.
2. Serve chilled immediately or keep in the freezer.

Nutritional Info Per Serving:
Calories:181kcal, Carbs:19g, Protein:2g, Fat:10g , Dietary Fiber:2g

Tropical Yogurt Panna Cotta

A zesty, panna cotta recipe made with yogurt and exotic fruits. The addition of gelatin not only enhances the texture but adds to the nutritional value of the desert as it is full of amino-acids, protein, and zinc.

Servings: 6

Total Cooking Time: 10 minutes

Ingredients:

- ½ cup of coconut milk
- 1 tbsp gelatin powder
- 2 ½ cups plain Greek yogurt
- 2 tbsp unsweetened coconut flakes
- 1 tbsp honey
- 1 ½ tsp vanilla extract
- ½ tsp ginger powder
- 1 large mango, diced

Method:
1. Dissolve the gelatin into 1.4 cups of coconut milk in a small mixing bowl. Allow softening for 1-2 minutes.
2. Add the remaining coconut milk to the saucepan and place over medium heat. Once the gelatin is done add the mixture to the saucepan.
3. Use a hand whisk to break down the gelatin until it is completely incorporated in the coconut milk. Bring to a boil and let boil for an extra 2 minutes.
4. Remove from the heat and add in the yogurt, honey, ginger powder, and vanilla extract.
5. Split the mixture into 6 small ramekins.

6. Let cool at room temperature and chill for at least 5 hours in the fridge before serving.
7. To serve, arrange a few slices of mango on top of each serving.

Nutritional Info Per Serving:
Calories:143kcal, Carbs:16.2g, Protein:7.8g, Fat: 5.7g, Dietary Fiber:1.5g

Date Paste

Ever wondered how to make date paste? This 2 ingredient recipe is all you need to make a sweet condiment that you can use as a jam or on top of other desserts.

Servings: 8

Total Cooking Time: 8 minutes

Ingredients:

- 16 oz. dates pitted
- 1 cup of boiling water

Method:

1. Soak the dated into a hot water bath for 5 minutes.
2. Add the dates with the water into a food processor and pulse on high speed for 3 minutes or until you achieve a paste-like consistency.
3. Store in the fridge for up to 2 months.

Conclusion

Now there is a natural way to combat anxiety and reduce your symptoms without relying on harsh pills that often come with side effects. In any case, though, it's best to consult your doctor when making any changes to your diet as some drugs may interfere with certain foods and cancel out their effect.

Keep in mind that the above recipes are targeted to those that suffer from mild anxiety chronically but they haven't reached a stage where their anxiety is really uncontrollable and needs more drastic treatments to be treated.

By following this diet and making a few healthy lifestyle changes that fit you and your schedule, you will feel tremendous relief from your anxiety symptoms.

We wish you all the best and good luck combating your anxiety with these special recipes and diet!

Made in the USA
Coppell, TX
13 September 2020